Challenge Yo

Check Out Our (

CW00402480

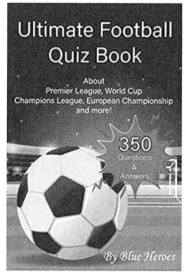

Ultimate Football Quiz Book

About
Premier League, World Cup
Champions League, European Championship
and more!

350
Questions
&
Answers

By Blue Heroes

Dive into the World of Football Thrilling Facts!

Knowledge is a powerful tool, and when it's about a subject as thrilling as football, learning becomes an absolute joy. Our Football Facts Book invites you to embrace the joy of discovery, encouraging you to explore the sport's intricacies with enthusiasm and curiosity.

We will appreciate it if you leave a review on Amazon.

B l u e   H e r o e s

Basic facts

Origin: Modern football originated in England in the mid-19th century. The rules of the game were codified in 1863 when the Football Association (The FA) was formed in England.

Objective: The primary objective of football is to score goals by getting the ball into the opposing team's net. The team with the most goals at the end of the match wins.

Number of Players: Each team consists of 11 players, including one goalkeeper. Substitutes can be made during the match, but typically only a certain number of substitutions are allowed.

Duration of the Game: A standard football match is played in two halves of 45 minutes each, with a 15-minute halftime interval.

The Ball: A spherical ball is used in football matches. The ball's circumference must be between 68 and 70 cm (27-28 inches), and its weight should be between 410 and 450 grams (14-16 ounces).

Basic facts

The Pitch: Football is played on a rectangular field with specific dimensions. The length of the field should be between 100-110 meters (110-120 yards), and the width should be between 64-75 meters (70-82 yards).

Fouls and Penalties: Certain actions, such as pushing, tripping, or handball, are considered fouls. The opposing team is awarded free kicks or penalties, depending on the location of the foul.

Offside Rule: A player is in an offside position if he is nearer to the opponent's goal line than both the ball and the second-to-last defender when the ball is played to him. Being in an offside position is not an offense in itself, but a player can be penalized for being offside if involved in active play.

Competitions: Football is played at various levels, from local leagues and school tournaments to international competitions like the FIFA World Cup, UEFA Champions League, and domestic leagues like the English Premier League and La Liga.

Basic facts

Global Popularity: Football is the world's most popular sport, played and watched by millions of people across the globe. It has a massive fan base and is followed passionately by fans from different cultures and backgrounds.

Throw-ins: When the ball goes out of play over the touchline, it is returned to the field via a throw-in. The thrower must keep both feet on the ground and deliver the ball from behind and over their head using both hands.

Goal Kicks: When the attacking team kicks the ball out over the defending team's goal line, a goal kick is awarded. The ball is placed in the six-yard box, and any player from the defending team can take the kick.

Corner Kicks: When the defending team kicks the ball out over their own goal line, the attacking team is awarded a corner kick. The ball is placed in the corner arc, and a player from the attacking team kicks it back into play.

Basic facts

Yellow and Red Cards: Referees can issue yellow cards as a warning for a serious foul or misconduct. Two yellow cards in the same match result in a red card, leading to the player being sent off. A direct red card can be given for a severe offense, and the team plays with one player less.

Injury Time: At the end of each half, the referee can add extra time to compensate for stoppages in play, usually due to injuries or time-wasting. This added time is commonly known as injury time or stoppage time.

Captains: Each team has a designated captain who wears an armband. The captain often serves as a team leader and has the privilege to discuss with the referee about on-field issues.

Rules: Football is governed by a set of rules known as the Laws of the Game. These rules are maintained by the International Football Association Board (IFAB) and are followed worldwide.

Advanced facts

Historical Roots: The origins of football can be traced back over 2,000 years, with various ancient civilizations playing games involving a ball and feet. The modern version of football, as we know it, evolved in the 19th century in England.

Laws of the Game: The Laws of the Game, maintained by the International Football Association Board (IFAB), serve as the rules for football worldwide. They are constantly reviewed and updated to ensure fairness and consistency in the sport.

FIFA World Cup: The FIFA World Cup, held every four years, is the most prestigious tournament in international football. The first World Cup was held in 1930, and Brazil has won the tournament a record five times.

Total Football: Coined by the Dutch in the 1970s, Total Football is a tactical theory where any outfield player can take over the role of any other player in a team. It emphasizes fluidity, positional awareness, and teamwork.

Advanced facts

Professional Leagues: Apart from the Premier League in England, there are several other top professional leagues around the world, such as La Liga in Spain, Serie A in Italy, Bundesliga in Germany, and Major League Soccer (MLS) in the United States and Canada.

Ballon d'Or: The Ballon d'Or is an annual football award presented by France Football magazine. It has been awarded since 1956 and is considered one of the most prestigious individual awards in the sport, given to the world's best male football player.

Football Records: Lionel Messi and Cristiano Ronaldo are two of the most prolific goal-scorers in football history. They have broken numerous records and have won multiple Ballon d'Or awards.

Women's Football: Women's football has been growing in popularity and recognition. The FIFA Women's World Cup, held every four years, is a significant tournament in women's football, and many countries have professional women's leagues.

Stadiums

Largest Stadium: Rungrado 1st of May Stadium in Pyongyang, North Korea, is the largest stadium in the world by capacity, with an official capacity of 114,000 spectators. It is primarily used for football and athletics events.

Wembley Stadium: Wembley Stadium in London, England, is one of the most famous football stadiums globally and has a seating capacity of 90,000. It has hosted numerous historic matches, including World Cup finals and the UEFA Champions League final.

Maracanã Stadium: Maracanã Stadium in Rio de Janeiro, Brazil, is an iconic venue. It hosted the 1950 FIFA World Cup final, which remains one of the most significant moments in football history.

Allianz Arena: Allianz Arena in Munich, Germany, is known for its striking illuminated facade that can change colors. It is the home stadium of FC Bayern Munich and TSV 1860 Munich.

Stadiums

Old Trafford: Old Trafford in Manchester, England, is the home of Manchester United. It is one of the most historic stadiums in football, known for its electrifying atmosphere during matches.

Camp Nou: Camp Nou in Barcelona, Spain, is the largest stadium in Europe by capacity and the home of FC Barcelona. It has a seating capacity of over 99,000 spectators.

Green Initiatives: Many modern stadiums are designed with sustainability in mind. They incorporate features like rainwater harvesting, solar panels, and energy-efficient lighting to minimize their environmental impact.

Multi-Purpose Arenas: Several stadiums around the world serve as multi-purpose arenas, hosting not only football matches but also concerts, sporting events, and other entertainment shows.

Stadium Architecture: Stadiums come in various architectural styles, from traditional bowl-shaped designs to modern, innovative structures. Architects often incorporate local culture and history into the stadium's design.

Stadiums

Stadium Expansion: Many stadiums undergo expansion and renovation projects to increase seating capacity and modernize facilities. These projects are often undertaken to meet the demands of growing fanbases and to enhance the overall fan experience.

Fanatical Atmosphere: Football stadiums are known for their passionate and vocal supporters. The energy and enthusiasm of the fans contribute significantly to the overall ambiance of the stadium during matches.

Stadium Names: Stadiums are often named after sponsors or notable figures in the club's history. The naming rights are sometimes sold to corporations, providing a significant source of revenue for the club.

Estadio Azteca: Situated in Mexico City, Mexico, Estadio Azteca is the first stadium to host two FIFA World Cup Finals (1970 and 1986). It is one of the most famous stadiums in the world.

VAR

Introduction: VAR is a technology introduced to assist on-field referees in making crucial decisions during football matches. It aims to reduce errors related to goals, penalties, red cards, and mistaken identity incidents.

First Implementation: VAR was officially used for the first time in a top-tier professional league during an A-League match in Australia on April 7, 2017. Its implementation in top European leagues followed soon after.

How VAR Works: VAR involves a team of video assistant referees who review incidents from multiple camera angles in real-time. They communicate with the on-field referee through an earpiece, providing advice on contentious decisions.

Types of Decisions Reviewed: VAR can be used for four types of decisions: goals, penalties, red cards, and mistaken identity in awarding cards. VAR checks for potential errors and ensures that the correct decision is made.

VAR

Goal Decisions: VAR checks for offside, handball, fouls, and other infringements in the build-up to a goal. If an offense is identified, the goal can be disallowed.

Penalty Decisions: VAR reviews penalty decisions, including fouls inside or outside the box. If a clear and obvious error is identified, the on-field referee can change the decision.

Red Card Decisions: VAR assists in reviewing incidents leading to red cards, ensuring that players are not unfairly sent off or that deserving players are not spared from a red card.

Mistaken Identity: VAR can correct instances where a wrong player is penalized, ensuring that the correct player receives the appropriate card.

VAR Challenges: In some leagues, each team has a limited number of VAR challenges per match. If a challenge is successful, the team retains their right to challenge again. If unsuccessful, they lose the challenge.

UEFA

Formation: UEFA was founded on June 15, 1954. It is the administrative and controlling body for European football.

Member Associations: UEFA has 55 member associations, representing national football governing bodies across Europe.

UEFA Competitions: UEFA organizes various prestigious club and national team competitions, including the UEFA Champions League, UEFA Europa League, UEFA European Championship (Euros), UEFA Nations League, and UEFA Women's Champions League.

UEFA Champions League: The UEFA Champions League is one of the most prestigious club competitions in the world. The tournament was established in 1955 and features the top clubs from European leagues competing for the title.

UEFA Respect Campaign:
UEFA runs the Respect campaign, promoting fair play, tolerance, and inclusion in football. The campaign encourages players, officials, and fans to respect opponents and the game.

UEFA

UEFA Europa League: Formerly known as the UEFA Cup, the UEFA Europa League is another major club competition. It was inaugurated in 1971 and is open to clubs finishing high in their respective national leagues.

UEFA European Championship (Euros): The UEFA European Championship, commonly referred to as the Euros, is the premier national team competition in Europe. It was first held in 1960 and is played every four years, featuring national teams from European countries.

UEFA Nations League: Introduced in 2018, the UEFA Nations League is a national team competition designed to improve the quality and competitiveness of international football matches for European national teams.

Fair Play: UEFA promotes fair play and respect on and off the field, encouraging sportsmanship and ethical conduct among players, officials, and fans.

UEFA

UEFA Women's Football: UEFA actively promotes women's football, organizing the UEFA Women's Champions League and supporting the development of women's football at the grassroots level.

UEFA Youth League: UEFA Youth League is a youth club competition that mirrors the UEFA Champions League. It provides young players with an opportunity to experience European competition at the youth level.

Financial Fair Play: UEFA has implemented Financial Fair Play regulations to promote financial stability and sustainable spending among football clubs in European competitions.

UEFA Headquarters: UEFA's headquarters are located in Nyon, Switzerland.

UEFA Grassroots Day: - UEFA Grassroots Day is an annual event promoting grassroots football across Europe. It encourages participation, fair play, and the joy of playing football from a young age.

FIFA

Formation: FIFA was founded on May 21, 1904, in Paris, France. It is the oldest international football organization.

Member Associations: FIFA has 211 member associations, making it one of the largest sports organizations in the world, encompassing national football governing bodies from almost every country.

FIFA World Cup: The FIFA World Cup is the most prestigious international football tournament. It has been held every four years since 1930, except in 1942 and 1946 due to World War II. The inaugural World Cup was hosted by Uruguay and won by the host nation.

Most World Cup Wins: Brazil holds the record for the most World Cup victories, with a total of five titles (1958, 1962, 1970, 1994, and 2002).

FIFA Women's World Cup: The FIFA Women's World Cup is the premier international competition in women's football. It has been held every four years since 1991.

FIFA

FIFA Ballon d'Or: FIFA awards the Ballon d'Or to the world's best male player and the FIFA Women's World Player of the Year to the best female player annually.

FIFA Confederations Cup: The FIFA Confederations Cup is held every four years, featuring national teams from around the world. It serves as a prelude to the upcoming World Cup and is a tournament of champions from different continents.

FIFA U-20 and U-17 World Cups: FIFA organizes international youth tournaments for players under 20 and under 17 years old, showcasing young talent from various countries.

FIFA Rankings: FIFA ranks national teams based on their performance in international competitions. These rankings are widely followed by fans and analysts.

FIFA Fair Play Award: FIFA presents the FIFA Fair Play Award to individuals, teams, or organizations that have made significant contributions to fair play and sportsmanship in football.

FIFA

FIFA World Rankings: FIFA publishes world rankings for national teams, providing a ranking system based on their performance in international matches.

FIFA Council: The FIFA Council is the main decision-making body of FIFA, responsible for setting policies, regulations, and the organization's overall direction.

FIFA Club World Cup: FIFA organizes the Club World Cup, an international club football tournament that features champion clubs from each of the six continental confederations, as well as the champion club from the host nation.

FIFA President: The current President of FIFA (as of my knowledge cutoff in September 2021) is Gianni Infantino. He assumed office in February 2016, succeeding Sepp Blatter.

FIFA Women's World Cup Expansion: FIFA expanded the Women's World Cup from 24 to 32 teams starting from the 2023 edition, allowing more nations to participate and promoting the growth of women's football globally.

FIFA

FIFA World Cup Trophy: The FIFA World Cup Trophy, awarded to the winners of the World Cup, is made of 18-carat gold and weighs around 6.1 kilograms (13.45 pounds). The original Jules Rimet Trophy was retired after Brazil won it for the third time in 1970.

FIFA Goal of the Year: FIFA awards the Puskás Award annually to the player, male or female, who is judged to have scored the most aesthetically significant and "most beautiful" goal of the year.

FIFA Beach Soccer World Cup: FIFA organizes the Beach Soccer World Cup, a tournament for national teams played on a beach or beach soccer-specific pitch. It has gained popularity as a unique and exciting form of football.

FIFA World Cup Host Selection: FIFA selects World Cup hosts through a bidding process where countries submit their proposals. The process involves rigorous evaluations, and the decision is made by the FIFA Congress.

World Cup

Inaugural World Cup: The first FIFA World Cup took place in Uruguay in 1930. Uruguay also won the tournament, becoming the first-ever World Cup champion.

Frequency: The World Cup is held every four years, except for 1942 and 1946 due to World War II. The next World Cup after 2022 will be in 2026.

Most Titles: Brazil holds the record for the most World Cup titles, with a total of five championships (1958, 1962, 1970, 1994, and 2002).

Jules Rimet Trophy: The original World Cup trophy was called the Jules Rimet Trophy, named after FIFA's third president. It was awarded from 1930 to 1970. Brazil's third World Cup victory in 1970 allowed them to keep the trophy permanently.

Top Scorer: Miroslav Klose of Germany holds the record for the most goals scored in World Cup history. He scored 16 goals in World Cup tournaments between 2002 and 2014.

World Cup

Host Countries: The World Cup has been hosted by 17 different countries. The 2022 World Cup will be hosted by Qatar, making it the first time the tournament will be held in the Middle East.

Youngest and Oldest Players: The youngest player to ever participate in a World Cup match is Pelé, who was 17 years and 239 days old when he played for Brazil in 1958. The oldest player to compete in the World Cup is Essam El-Hadary of Egypt, who was 45 years and 161 days old in 2018.

Maracanã Stadium: The Maracanã Stadium in Rio de Janeiro, Brazil, is one of the most iconic World Cup venues. It hosted the 1950 World Cup final, where Uruguay defeated Brazil in a match famously known as the "Maracanazo."

VAR Implementation: The 2018 World Cup in Russia was the first tournament where Video Assistant Referee (VAR) technology was officially used to assist match officials in decision-making.

World Cup

VAR in Penalties: VAR was used for the first time in a World Cup penalty shootout during the 2018 tournament. France and Australia were awarded penalties after VAR reviews in their respective matches.

VAR Offside Technology: VAR uses advanced technology to determine offside decisions, ensuring accurate calls in situations where goals are scored from close-range plays.

Perfect Qualification Record: Brazil is the only nation that has appeared in every World Cup since the tournament's inception in 1930.

Most Goals in a Single Tournament: Just Fontaine of France holds the record for the most goals scored in a single World Cup tournament. He scored 13 goals in the 1958 World Cup held in Sweden.

Fastest Hat-Trick: Hungarian player László Kiss holds the record for the fastest hat-trick in World Cup history. He scored three goals in just 7 minutes during a match against El Salvador in 1982.

World Cup

Defending Champions' Curse: No team has successfully defended the World Cup title since Brazil in 1962. The defending champions have often struggled in the subsequent tournaments.

Fewest Goals in a Tournament: The 1990 World Cup in Italy saw the fewest goals scored per game, with an average of 2.21 goals per match.

First African World Cup: The 1934 World Cup in Italy did not feature any African teams. The first African team to qualify for the World Cup was Egypt in 1934, although they withdrew from the tournament.

Multiple Host Countries: The 2002 World Cup in South Korea and Japan was the first to be co-hosted by two countries from different confederations. It was also the first World Cup held in Asia.

Most Final Losses: Germany and Argentina share the record for the most World Cup final losses. Both teams have lost in the final match of the tournament on four occasions.

World Cup

VAR's Impact: The implementation of VAR (Video Assistant Referee) technology has led to more accurate decisions, reducing controversies and enhancing the overall fairness of the matches.

Host Country Advantage: Historically, host countries have often performed well in the World Cup. The supportive home crowd and familiarity with local conditions provide a significant advantage to the host nation's team.

Most Consecutive Titles: Italy and Brazil share the record for the most consecutive World Cup titles. Both teams won the tournament twice in a row - Italy in 1934 and 1938, and Brazil in 1958 and 1962.

Oldest and Youngest Goal Scorers: Roger Milla of Cameroon is the oldest goal scorer in World Cup history, scoring a goal at the age of 42 years and 39 days during the 1994 World Cup. Pelé of Brazil is the youngest goal scorer, finding the net at the age of 17 years and 239 days during the 1958 World Cup.

UEFA European Championship

Inaugural Tournament: The first UEFA European Championship was held in 1960. The Soviet Union won the inaugural tournament, defeating Yugoslavia in the final.
Frequency: The European Championship is held every four years. The competition features national teams from Europe and is one of the most prestigious international tournaments in football.
Number of Teams: Initially, the tournament featured only four teams in the final tournament. Since 1996, the number of participating teams has increased. In Euro 2016, 24 teams competed for the title.
Most Titles: Germany and Spain share the record for the most European Championship titles, with three each. Germany won in 1972, 1980, and 1996, while Spain won in 1964, 2008, and 2012.

UEFA European Championship

Golden Boot: The Golden Boot award is given to the top goal scorer of the tournament. Michel Platini of France holds the record for the most goals scored in a single European Championship edition, netting nine goals in 1984.

Host Nations: The tournament has been hosted by various European countries. The upcoming Euro 2024 will be hosted by Germany.

Denmark's Surprise Victory: In 1992, Denmark was not originally qualified for the tournament. Due to political turmoil in Yugoslavia, Denmark was invited to replace them. Surprisingly, Denmark went on to win the tournament, defeating Germany in the final.

Greece's Unexpected Win: In 2004, Greece won their first major international trophy by clinching the European Championship. They defeated the host nation, Portugal, in the final.

UEFA European Championship

Penalty Shootouts: If a knockout stage match ends in a draw, it goes into extra time. If the match remains tied after extra time, it is decided by a penalty shootout.

European Championship Expansion: The tournament was expanded to 16 teams in 1996, and further expanded to 24 teams in 2016. This expansion allowed more teams to participate and increased the excitement of the tournament.

VAR Implementation: Similar to the FIFA World Cup, the UEFA European Championship also adopted the Video Assistant Referee (VAR) technology to aid match officials in making correct decisions on the field.

Final Venues: The final matches of the European Championship have been held in renowned stadiums across Europe, including Wembley Stadium in London, Stade de France in Paris, and Estádio da Luz in Lisbon, among others.

UEFA European Championship

Team of the Tournament: UEFA selects a "Team of the Tournament," featuring the best-performing players from various positions during the competition.

Football Legacy: The European Championship has become a significant part of Europe's football legacy, showcasing the talent and passion of European footballers and uniting fans from different nations.

Longest-Unbeaten Run: Spain holds the record for the longest unbeaten run in the history of the European Championship. They went unbeaten for 14 matches from 2008 to 2016, winning three consecutive tournaments (2008, 2010 World Cup, 2012).

Top Scorer: Cristiano Ronaldo is the all-time top scorer in the history of the European Championship. He achieved this record during Euro 2020, surpassing Michel Platini's record of nine goals.

UEFA European Championship

Oldest Goal Scorer: Ivica Vastić of Austria is the oldest goal scorer in the history of the European Championship. He scored a penalty against Poland during Euro 2008 at the age of 38 years and 257 days.

Most Appearances: Germany and Russia share the record for the most appearances in the final tournament without winning the trophy. Both teams have appeared four times in the final without securing the title.

Czechoslovakia's Historic Win: Czechoslovakia won the European Championship in 1976, becoming the first team from outside Western Europe to win the tournament. They defeated West Germany in the final.

First Golden Goal: The concept of the "Golden Goal" (sudden death extra time) was first introduced in the European Championship. Oliver Bierhoff of Germany scored the first Golden Goal against the Czech Republic in the final of Euro 1996.

UEFA European Championship

Multiple Host Cities: Euro 2020 (held in 2021 due to the pandemic) was the first tournament to be hosted in multiple cities across different European countries. It was hosted in 11 cities from 11 different countries.

Michel Platini's Record Goals in One Tournament: Michel Platini scored nine goals in Euro 1984, a record for the most goals in a single European Championship tournament. He achieved this feat in just five matches.

Cristiano Ronaldo's Milestone Goals: Cristiano Ronaldo became the first player to score in four different European Championships (2004, 2008, 2012, 2016, and 2020). He also became the first player to play in five European Championships.

France's Back-to-Back Wins: France won back-to-back European Championships in 1984 and 2000. They defeated Spain in 1984 and Italy in 2000 to claim the titles.

UEFA Champions League

Inauguration: The UEFA Champions League, originally known as the European Cup, was inaugurated in the 1955-1956 season. The first winners were Real Madrid, and they went on to win the first five editions of the tournament.

Format: The Champions League involves several qualifying rounds, followed by a group stage with 32 teams. The top two teams from each group advance to the knockout stages, culminating in a single-match final.

Most Titles: Real Madrid holds the record for the most Champions League titles, with 13 wins. They won their 13th title in the 2017-2018 season.

Consecutive Titles: Real Madrid holds the record for winning the Champions League consecutively. They achieved this feat from 1955-1956 to 1957-1958 and from 2015-2016 to 2017-2018.

UEFA Champions League

Final Venue: The final of the Champions League is held in a different stadium each year. Some notable venues include Wembley Stadium in London, Camp Nou in Barcelona, and San Siro in Milan.

Fastest Final Goal: Paolo Maldini of AC Milan scored the fastest goal in a Champions League final. He found the net just 50 seconds into the 2005 final against Liverpool.

Comeback in the Final: Liverpool holds the record for the most significant comeback in a Champions League final. They trailed 3-0 at halftime against AC Milan in the 2005 final but came back to win the match on penalties.

Top Scorer: Cristiano Ronaldo is the all-time top scorer in the Champions League. He has scored numerous goals for Manchester United, Real Madrid, and Juventus in the tournament.

UEFA Champions League

First British Club to Win: Celtic FC was the first British club to win the European Cup in 1967, defeating Inter Milan in the final.

Invincibles: In the 1972-1973 season, Ajax became the first club to go through a European Cup campaign unbeaten. They won the title without losing a single match.

Youngest Finalist: Raúl of Real Madrid holds the record for being the youngest player to appear in a Champions League final. He played in the 1998 final against Juventus at the age of 20 years and 4 months.

Goals in a Single Season: Lionel Messi holds the record for the most goals scored in a single Champions League season. He scored 14 goals in the 2011-2012 season.

VAR Implementation: Video Assistant Referee (VAR) technology was introduced in the knockout stages of the Champions League to assist match officials in making accurate decisions.

Managers

Oldest Manager: The oldest football manager in professional football history is Jock Wallace. He managed Colchester United at the age of 74 in 1992.

Youngest Premier League Manager: At the age of 33 years and 41 days, Frank Lampard became the youngest manager in the history of the English Premier League when he took charge of Derby County in 2018.

Longest Managerial Tenure: Sir Alex Ferguson holds the record for the longest managerial tenure at a single club in English football. He managed Manchester United for 26 years from 1986 to 2013.

Most Successful Manager: Sir Alex Ferguson is widely regarded as one of the most successful managers in football history. He won 49 major trophies during his managerial career, including 13 Premier League titles and 2 UEFA Champions League titles with Manchester United.

Managers

First Foreign Manager in England: Jozef Vengloš from Czechoslovakia became the first foreign manager in English football when he took charge of Aston Villa in 1990.

Pep Guardiola's Records: Pep Guardiola has achieved numerous records as a manager, including guiding Barcelona to a sextuple in 2009 (winning six major trophies in a single calendar year) and Manchester City to the first-ever English domestic treble in 2019 (Premier League, FA Cup, and League Cup).

First Female Manager in Men's Football League: Helena Costa became the first female manager of a professional men's team in France when she was appointed as the manager of Clermont Foot in 2014.

Mourinho's Success: José Mourinho is known for his quick success at clubs. He won the league title in his first season with Porto, Chelsea (in his first spell), Inter Milan, and Real Madrid.

Managers

Guardiola's Tiki-Taka: Pep Guardiola popularized the "tiki-taka" style of play during his time at Barcelona, emphasizing short passing and movement, which led to great success for the team.

Football Manager Video Game: The Football Manager video game series, created by Sports Interactive, allows players to take on the role of a football manager, making decisions about tactics, transfers, and more. It has a large following among football fans and even some professional managers use it for scouting.

International Success: Vicente del Bosque became the only manager to win the World Cup, European Championship, and Champions League. He achieved this feat with Spain, Real Madrid, and the Spanish national team, respectively.

Sir Matt Busby: Sir Matt Busby is remembered as one of the greatest managers in Manchester United's history. He rebuilt the team after the Munich air disaster in 1958 and led them to their first European Cup triumph in 1968.

Managers

Managerial Trophies: Sir Alex Ferguson holds the record for the most English league titles (13) by a single manager. He managed Aberdeen and Manchester United during his illustrious career.

First Black Manager in England: Keith Alexander was the first black manager in the English Football League. He managed Lincoln City from 1993 to 1994.

Youngest Premier League Manager to Win the Title: At the age of 36, Brian Clough managed Nottingham Forest to the English First Division title in 1978. This achievement still stands as the youngest managerial age for a top-flight English league title.

The 36-Hour Interview: Marcelo Bielsa, the Argentine manager known for his meticulous approach to the game, reportedly conducted a 36-hour interview with the Chilean club, Universidad de Chile, to discuss his tactics and plans for the team before taking over as their manager.

National teams

Oldest National Team: The oldest national football team in the world is England. They played their first international match against Scotland in 1872.

World Cup Dominance: Brazil is the only national team to have appeared in every World Cup since the tournament's inception in 1930. They have also won the World Cup a record five times.

Most World Cup Titles: Brazil holds the record for the most World Cup titles, with a total of five championships (1958, 1962, 1970, 1994, and 2002).

Youngest World Cup Winners: Pelé of Brazil became the youngest player to win a World Cup when he lifted the trophy at the age of 17 in 1958.

Fastest World Cup Goal: Hakan Şükür of Turkey scored the fastest goal in World Cup history, finding the net just 11 seconds into a match against South Korea in the 2002 World Cup

National teams

Longest Unbeaten Run: The Spanish national team holds the record for the longest unbeaten run in international football. They went 35 consecutive matches without a loss between 2006 and 2009.

Most Goals in a World Cup Tournament: Just Fontaine of France holds the record for the most goals scored in a single World Cup tournament. He scored 13 goals in the 1958 World Cup in Sweden.

Oldest World Cup Player: The oldest player to participate in a World Cup match is Essam El-Hadary of Egypt. He was 45 years and 161 days old when he played in the 2018 World Cup.

Most European Championship Titles: Germany and Spain share the record for the most UEFA European Championship titles, with three each.

Top Scorer in International Matches: Ali Daei of Iran holds the record for the most goals scored in international matches. He scored 109 goals for Iran in his international career.

National teams

Highest FIFA Ranking: The highest FIFA ranking ever achieved by a national team is 1st. Several teams, including Brazil, Germany, Spain, and France, have reached the top spot.

Lowest FIFA Ranking: The lowest FIFA ranking ever achieved by a national team is 211th. Bhutan and San Marino share this position.

Unbeaten Streaks: Several national teams have impressive unbeaten streaks in international football, showcasing their dominance in specific eras.

Fair Play: FIFA awards the Fair Play Trophy to national teams that have demonstrated outstanding sportsmanship and fair play during international competitions.

Netherlands' Total Football: The Dutch national team popularized the concept of "Total Football," an attacking style of play where players are versatile and can switch positions seamlessly. This approach was prominent during the 1974 FIFA World Cup.

Kits

Origins: Football kits were first introduced in the late 1800s. Initially, players wore their own clothes, but this led to confusion on the field. Teams started wearing matching outfits to distinguish themselves.

Design Evolution: Football kits have evolved significantly over the years. Early kits were made of heavy materials like wool. Today, they are made of lightweight, breathable, and moisture-wicking materials like polyester.

Home and Away Kits: Teams have home and away kits to avoid clashes with the opposing team's colors. The home kit is the primary one, and the away kit is worn when playing away matches.

Third Kits: Some teams also have a third kit, which is used when both the home and away kits clash with the opponent's uniforms. These kits often have unique designs and colors.

Crests and Logos: Football kits feature the team's crest, which is a symbol of the club. The crest represents the club's identity and is often a source of pride for fans.

Kits

Sponsorship: Football kits often feature sponsorship logos from companies or brands. Sponsorship deals can be highly lucrative for football clubs and contribute significantly to their revenue.

Kit Manufacturers: Major sportswear companies like Nike, Adidas, Puma, and Under Armour manufacture football kits. These companies sign contracts with clubs to provide their kits.

Kit Launches: Football clubs often organize elaborate events to unveil their new kits for the upcoming season. These launches are attended by players, managers, and fans and are highly anticipated events.

Jersey Numbers: Players' jersey numbers are also a crucial part of the kit. Certain numbers have iconic status, and players often have personal preferences or superstitions regarding their jersey numbers.

Kits

Limited Editions: Some clubs release limited edition or commemorative kits to celebrate specific events, anniversaries, or achievements. These kits are often collector's items among fans.

Cultural Significance: Football kits have cultural significance and can represent the identity and history of a club. The colors, patterns, and designs often have historical and local meanings.

Jersey Swaps: After matches, it's a common tradition for players to exchange jerseys as a sign of mutual respect. These exchanged jerseys are often prized possessions for fans and collectors.

Unique Patterns: In 1996, Germany introduced a revolutionary kit with a design that was not just a solid color. It featured a series of black, red, and yellow stripes, breaking away from the traditional solid-color designs.

Ball

Standard Size: A regulation football, as defined by FIFA, must have a circumference (around the ball) of 68-70 cm (27-28 inches) and a weight of 410-450 grams (14-16 ounces) at the start of the match.

Design Changes: The traditional black-and-white paneled design of footballs, known as the "Buckminster Ball" or "Tango," was first introduced in the 1970 FIFA World Cup. Since then, various designs and technologies have been used for different tournaments and leagues.

Material: Footballs are typically made from leather or other synthetic materials. Modern footballs often use synthetic materials because they are more durable and perform consistently in different weather conditions.

Inside Structure: The inside of a football contains layers of fabric and latex or rubber bladders. The bladders hold the air and give the ball its shape and bounce.

Ball

Waterproofing: Traditional leather footballs could become significantly heavier when wet, affecting the game. Modern footballs have waterproof layers to prevent them from absorbing water, ensuring consistent weight and performance in all weather conditions.

Aerodynamics: The design and panel arrangement of a football significantly affect its flight path. Engineers study aerodynamics to ensure the ball's stability and predictability during a match.

Manufacturers: Major sports equipment companies like Adidas, Nike, and Puma are renowned for producing high-quality footballs. Each World Cup often features a unique ball design created by the official manufacturer.

High-Tech Balls: In recent years, advanced technologies, such as embedded microchips and sensors, have been used in footballs for tracking speed, spin, and other metrics during professional matches and training.

Ball

Altitude Adjustment: FIFA introduced the "Teamgeist" ball for the 2006 World Cup, which had a reduced number of panels. This design was meant to minimize the effect of air pressure changes at different altitudes.

Scented Footballs: Some manufacturers produce scented footballs. The scent is usually added to the rubber or leather used in the ball and can range from vanilla to fruit scents.

Testing Protocols: Footballs undergo rigorous testing procedures to ensure they meet the required standards. These tests include measurements for size, weight, shape, and roundness.

Symbol of Unity: Footballs have become a universal symbol of unity and friendship. Players often exchange signed footballs after matches, and fans collect autographed balls as cherished memorabilia.

High-Tech GPS Footballs: In modern training sessions, footballs equipped with GPS technology are used to track players' movements, passes, and other statistics during practice.

Field

Standard Dimensions: A standard football field, as defined by FIFA, should have a length (touchline) of 100-110 meters (110-120 yards) and a width (goal line) of 64-75 meters (70-82 yards). The penalty area extends 16.5 meters (18 yards) from each goal post and 40.3 meters (44 yards) in width.

Halfway Line: The halfway line divides the field into two equal halves. It is a crucial line used to restart the game after goals, at the beginning of each half, and after stoppages.

Goalposts: The goalposts are located at the center of each goal line. They consist of two upright posts, which must be 7.32 meters (8 feet) apart, and a horizontal crossbar positioned 2.44 meters (8 feet) above the ground.

Corner Arc: The corner arc is a quarter-circle with a radius of 1 meter (1 yard) drawn at each corner of the field. Corners are taken from within this arc.

Field

Penalty Spot: The penalty spot is located 11 meters (12 yards) from the center of the goal. Penalties are taken from this spot during matches.

Centre Circle: The center circle has a radius of 9.15 meters (10 yards) and is located at the midpoint of the halfway line. The opposing team must be outside this circle during kick-offs.

Goal Area: The goal area, commonly known as the six-yard box, extends 5.5 meters (6 yards) from each goal post and 16.5 meters (18 yards) in width. Goalkeepers can handle the ball within this area.

Technical Area: Each team has a designated technical area where coaches and substitutes are positioned during the match. This area is located along the edge of the pitch.

Floodlights: Many football fields, especially those used for evening matches, are equipped with floodlights to ensure adequate visibility for players and spectators.

Gate & Goal

Standard Size: Football goals are standard-sized structures with an opening that measures 7.32 meters (8 feet) in height and 2.44 meters (8 feet) in width. These measurements are set by FIFA and are consistent across professional and international matches.

Goal Nets: The goalposts are typically equipped with netting to catch and show when a goal has been scored. The net must be appropriately attached to the goalposts and crossbar.

Goalkeeper's Territory: Goalkeepers are the only players allowed to use their hands and arms to play the ball, but only within their penalty area. If they venture out of this area and handle the ball, it results in a free kick for the opposing team.

Golden Goal Rule: In the past, some football tournaments implemented the Golden Goal rule, where the first team to score in extra time would instantly win the match. This rule is no longer used in most competitions.

Gate & Goal

Goal Decision System (Goal-Line Technology): To avoid controversial goal decisions, many modern football leagues and tournaments use goal-line technology. This system uses cameras to determine whether the entire ball has crossed the goal line, helping referees make accurate decisions about whether a goal has been scored.

Goal Celebrations: Scoring a goal is a moment of immense joy for players and fans alike. Players often celebrate by running to the corner flag, performing choreographed dances, or huddling with teammates. Elaborate goal celebrations have become a significant part of the sport's entertainment.

Home and Away Goals: In some tournaments, when matches are played over two legs, away goals can have extra significance. If the aggregate score is tied, the team with more goals scored away from home advances.

Own Goals: If a defensive player accidentally scores a goal in their team's net, it's called an own goal. Own goals can significantly impact the outcome of a match.

Memorable goals

Diego Maradona's "Hand of God" and "Goal of the Century" (1986): In the 1986 FIFA World Cup quarter-final between Argentina and England, Maradona scored two of the most famous goals in football history. The first, known as the "Hand of God," involved Maradona using his hand to punch the ball into the net. The second goal, the "Goal of the Century," saw him dribble past five English outfield players to score.

Zinedine Zidane's Volley in the UEFA Champions League Final (2002): Zidane's stunning left-footed volley for Real Madrid against Bayer Leverkusen in the 2002 UEFA Champions League final is often regarded as one of the greatest goals in the competition's history.

Gareth Bale's Solo Run in Copa del Rey Final (2014): Bale's solo run from the halfway line for Real Madrid against Barcelona in the Copa del Rey final showcased his incredible speed and skill. He outran Barça's Marc Bartra and slotted the ball into the net.

Memorable goals

Marco van Basten's Volley in the UEFA European Championship Final (1988): Van Basten scored a spectacular volley from an acute angle for the Netherlands against the Soviet Union in the final of the 1988 UEFA European Championship. The goal is considered one of the best goals ever scored in a major tournament final.

Roberto Carlos' Free-Kick against France (1997): In a friendly match between Brazil and France, Roberto Carlos scored a seemingly impossible free-kick from a wide angle. The ball curved dramatically, leaving spectators and players in awe.

Michael Owen's Solo Goal against Argentina (1998): In the 1998 FIFA World Cup, Michael Owen scored a memorable solo goal for England against Argentina, showcasing his speed, dribbling ability, and composure in front of goal.

Memorable goals

Dennis Bergkamp's Touch and Finish (1998): Bergkamp's goal for the Netherlands against Argentina in the 1998 World Cup quarter-final displayed extraordinary ball control. He trapped a long pass with one touch, turned the defender with another, and slotted the ball into the net with precision.

Steven Gerrard's Long-Range Goal against West Ham (2006): Gerrard's goal in the 2006 FA Cup final for Liverpool against West Ham United, a powerful shot from outside the box, helped his team equalize and eventually win the trophy.

Sergio Aguero's Title-Winning Goal (2012): Aguero scored the winning goal for Manchester City against Queens Park Rangers on the final day of the 2011-2012 Premier League season, securing City's first league title in 44 years in dramatic fashion.

Andres Iniesta's World Cup Final Goal (2010): Iniesta scored the winning goal for Spain in the 2010 FIFA World Cup final against the Netherlands, securing Spain's first-ever World Cup trophy.

Memorable goals

Arjen Robben's Solo Goal against Spain (2014): In the 2014 FIFA World Cup, Arjen Robben scored a crucial solo goal for the Netherlands against Spain. His electrifying run past multiple defenders showcased his speed and skill.

Rivaldo's Bicycle Kick Goal (1999): Playing for Barcelona against Valencia in La Liga, Rivaldo scored a stunning bicycle kick goal. The acrobatic strike showcased his technical brilliance and athleticism.

Wayne Rooney vs Manchester City (2011): Rooney's bicycle kick goal for Manchester United against Manchester City in the Manchester derby was a stunning display of athleticism and technique. It proved to be the match-winning goal.

Robin van Persie vs Aston Villa (2013): Van Persie's volley for Manchester United against Aston Villa demonstrated incredible technique. He connected with the ball mid-air, sending it into the net with precision.

Long-range goals

Scoring Beyond Halfway Line: Goals scored from beyond the halfway line are referred to as "long-range goals." These goals are often celebrated due to the precision and power required to beat the goalkeeper from such a distance.

David Beckham's Iconic Goal: One of the most famous long-range goals was scored by David Beckham for Manchester United against Wimbledon in 1996. Beckham noticed the opposing goalkeeper off his line and scored from the halfway line, marking one of the earliest and most iconic instances of this type of goal.

Xabi Alonso's Halfway Line Goal: Xabi Alonso scored a remarkable goal from the halfway line for Liverpool against Newcastle United in 2006. His strike caught the Newcastle goalkeeper off guard, leading to one of the most celebrated long-distance goals in Premier League history.

Long-range goals

Goalkeeper's Nightmare: Long-range goals are often considered a goalkeeper's nightmare because the ball travels with great speed and can change direction, making it difficult to predict and save.

Technique Matters: Scoring from a distance requires excellent technique. Players must strike the ball cleanly and accurately, ensuring it has the right amount of power and swerve to beat the goalkeeper.

Team Effort: Long-range goals can also be a result of teamwork. Players may create space for a teammate with a powerful long-range shot, hoping for a deflection or rebound opportunity in case the initial shot is saved.

Famous Free-Kick Goals: Many long-range goals come from free-kicks. Players like Cristiano Ronaldo, Lionel Messi, and Roberto Carlos are known for their ability to score from considerable distances, bending the ball around the defensive wall.

Long-range goals

Gerrard's Hat-Trick of Long-Range Goals:
Steven Gerrard scored three long-range goals in one match against Everton in the 2011-2012 season, earning him a memorable hat-trick and solidifying his status as a Liverpool legend.

Longest Recorded Goal: As of my last update in September 2021, the longest recorded goal in the Premier League was scored by Charlie Adam. He netted a goal from approximately 66.44 meters (or 219 feet) for Stoke City against Chelsea in 2015.

Le Tissier's Long-Range Prowess: Matt Le Tissier, who played for Southampton, was a master of long-range goals. He was known for his ability to score from distances that seemed impossible, often surprising goalkeepers with his accuracy.

Scorpion Kick Against Italy (2004): While playing for Sweden against Italy, Ibrahimovic executed a scorpion kick to score an astonishing goal. This acrobatic move became one of his signature goals.

Memorable saves

Gordon Banks' Save against Pele (1970): In the 1970 World Cup, England's goalkeeper Gordon Banks made a legendary save against Pele's powerful header. Despite Pele's header seeming destined for the net, Banks made an incredible diving save to deny the Brazilian striker, which is often regarded as one of the greatest saves in football history.

Jerzy Dudek's Double Save in the 2005 Champions League Final: In the penalty shootout of the 2005 UEFA Champions League final between Liverpool and AC Milan, Liverpool's goalkeeper Jerzy Dudek made two crucial saves against Andriy Shevchenko. His saves helped Liverpool win the shootout and secure their fifth European Cup title.

Keylor Navas' Saves in the 2014 World Cup: Costa Rica's goalkeeper Keylor Navas was a standout performer in the 2014 FIFA World Cup. He made several crucial saves, including a memorable one against Greece in the Round of 16 match, helping Costa Rica advance to the quarter-finals.

Memorable saves

David Seaman's Save against Paul Peschisolido (2003): In the FA Cup semi-final between Arsenal and Sheffield United, David Seaman made a fantastic save to deny Paul Peschisolido's close-range header. Seaman's save was crucial in securing Arsenal's spot in the final.

Luis Arconada's Save in the Euro 1984 Final: In the final of the 1984 UEFA European Championship between France and Spain, Spanish goalkeeper Luis Arconada made a rare error by letting Michel Platini's free-kick slip under him. This mistake proved costly as France won the match. Despite the error, Arconada remains one of the greatest Spanish goalkeepers of all time.

David De Gea's Saves in the Premier League: Manchester United's goalkeeper David De Gea has made numerous spectacular saves in the Premier League, earning him a reputation as one of the best goalkeepers in the world. His quick reflexes and acrobatic saves have often rescued his team from difficult situations.

Memorable saves

Rene Higuita's Scorpion Kick Save (1995): Colombian goalkeeper Rene Higuita executed a famous "scorpion kick" save against England in a friendly match at Wembley Stadium. Higuita cleared the ball using his heels while diving forward, creating one of the most unconventional and memorable saves in football history.

Alisson Becker's Last-Minute Save in the Champions League (2019): In the 2018-2019 UEFA Champions League semi-final second leg between Liverpool and Barcelona, Alisson Becker made a crucial last-minute save against Lionel Messi's close-range header. Liverpool went on to win the tie and eventually clinched the Champions League title.

Tim Howard's Record-Breaking Saves in a World Cup Match: American goalkeeper Tim Howard set a World Cup record by making 15 saves in a single match during the 2014 World Cup Round of 16 match against Belgium. Despite the loss, Howard's performance was widely praised.

Premier League

Inauguration: The Premier League was founded on February 20, 1992, when clubs in the Football League First Division broke away from the Football League to form their own league.

Clubs: There are 20 clubs in the Premier League. Each team plays 38 matches in a season – 19 home and 19 away.

Popularity: It is one of the most-watched football leagues globally and is broadcast in 212 territories to 643 million homes.

Record Title Wins: Manchester United has won the most Premier League titles (13), followed by Manchester City and Chelsea.

Top Scorers: Alan Shearer holds the record for the most Premier League goals, scoring 260 goals during his career.

Financial Power: Premier League clubs are some of the wealthiest in the world, attracting top talents and managers due to high revenue from broadcasting rights and sponsorships.

Premier League

Most Titles in a Row: Manchester United and Chelsea share the record for winning the league title in consecutive seasons – three times in a row.

Global Fanbase: The Premier League has a massive global fanbase. Fans from around the world follow their favorite teams and players passionately.

Competitive Nature: The league is known for its unpredictability and competitiveness. Any team can win on any given matchday, making it exciting for fans.

First Champions: The first Premier League champions were Manchester United. They clinched the title in the inaugural 1992-1993 season.

Television Rights: The sale of television broadcasting rights significantly contributed to the financial success of the league. It is broadcast in over 200 countries, reaching millions of viewers globally.

Premier League

Trophies: The Premier League champions are awarded the Premier League Trophy. There are also individual awards such as the Golden Boot for the league's top scorer and the Player of the Season award.

Community Work: The Premier League is involved in various community programs and initiatives, supporting charitable causes and promoting football at the grassroots level.

Golden Goal Rule: The Golden Goal rule, where the first team to score in extra time would win, was briefly implemented in the Premier League during the 1994-1995 and 1995-1996 seasons. It was later abandoned.

Leicester City's Unlikely Title Win: Leicester City's triumph in the 2015-2016 season is widely regarded as one of the greatest underdog stories in football. They were 5000-1 outsiders to win the league at the start of the season.

First Foreign Manager: Arsène Wenger, who managed Arsenal, was the first foreign manager to win the Premier League title. He achieved this feat in the 1997-1998 season.

Premier League

First season

Inception: The Premier League officially began on August 15, 1992. The first matchday saw Sheffield United draw 2-2 with Manchester United, and Sheffield Wednesday beat Everton 2-1.

Number of Teams: In the first season, there were 22 teams competing in the Premier League. The number was reduced to 20 in the following season (1993-1994).

First Champions: Manchester United was the inaugural Premier League champion. They secured the title on April 10, 1993, with several matches to spare.

Top Scorer: Teddy Sheringham of Tottenham Hotspur was the top scorer of the inaugural Premier League season with 22 goals.

Television Broadcast: The introduction of the Premier League also brought a significant increase in television broadcasting rights revenue. Sky Sports became the major broadcaster, helping the league gain widespread coverage.

Premier League

First season

Final Standings: Manchester United finished the season at the top of the table with 84 points, 10 points ahead of second-placed Aston Villa.

Player of the Season: The first-ever Premier League Player of the Season award was given to Teddy Sheringham for his outstanding performances during the 1992-1993 season.

Fair Play: The Premier League introduced the Fair Play League in its first season, rewarding teams for good behavior on the pitch. The team with the best fair play record received a spot in the UEFA Cup.

First Premier League Goal: The first-ever goal in the Premier League was scored by Sheffield United's Brian Deane. He found the net just five minutes into the match against Manchester United on August 15, 1992.

First Hat-Trick: Eric Cantona, playing for Leeds United, scored the first hat-trick in the Premier League on September 25, 1992, against Tottenham Hotspur.

Serie A

Inauguration: Serie A was inaugurated in 1898, making it one of the oldest football leagues in the world.

Number of Teams: Serie A typically consists of 20 teams competing for the league title each season.

Juventus Dominance: Juventus is the most successful club in Serie A history, having won the league title multiple times. They have had periods of extraordinary dominance, especially in recent years, winning multiple consecutive league titles.

AC Milan and Inter Milan Rivalry: The Milan Derby, or Derby della Madonnina, is one of the most intense and historic rivalries in Serie A. AC Milan and Inter Milan are the two major teams in the city, and their matches are highly anticipated by fans worldwide.

Top Scorer: Silvio Piola holds the record for the most goals scored in Serie A. He scored 274 goals while playing for Pro Vercelli, Lazio, and Juventus.

Serie A

Multiple Titles: Several legendary players have graced Serie A, including Paolo Maldini, Roberto Baggio, Gabriel Batistuta, Alessandro Del Piero, and Francesco Totti, all of whom have won multiple league titles.

AC Milan's Invincible Season: AC Milan went unbeaten in the 1991-1992 Serie A season, winning the league title with 22 wins and 12 draws.

Inter Milan's Treble: Inter Milan achieved an incredible treble in the 2009-2010 season under coach José Mourinho. They won the Serie A title, the Coppa Italia, and the UEFA Champions League.

High-Scoring Matches: Serie A is known for its defensive style, but it has also seen high-scoring matches. The league has produced legendary strikers such as Gabriel Batistuta, Marco van Basten, and Paolo Rossi.

Most Titles: Juventus holds the record for the most Serie A titles. The club has won the league championship numerous times, establishing itself as one of Italy's most successful teams.

La Liga

Inauguration: La Liga was founded in 1929. The inaugural season took place in 1929-1930.

Number of Teams: La Liga typically consists of 20 teams competing for the league title each season.

El Clásico: The matches between Real Madrid and Barcelona, known as El Clásico, are one of the most intense and watched football rivalries in the world.

Top Scorer: Lionel Messi holds the record for the most goals scored in a single La Liga season. He scored 50 goals for Barcelona in the 2011-2012 season.

Pichichi Trophy: The Pichichi Trophy is awarded to the top goal scorer of each La Liga season. It is named after the legendary Athletic Bilbao striker Rafael "Pichichi" Moreno.

Real Madrid's Success: Real Madrid is the most successful club in La Liga history, having won the league title numerous times. They have also had remarkable success in European competitions.

La Liga

European Dominance: Spanish clubs, particularly Real Madrid and Barcelona, have a strong presence in European competitions. They have consistently performed well in the UEFA Champions League and UEFA Europa League.

Barcelona's Tiki-Taka: FC Barcelona, especially during the era under Pep Guardiola, popularized the "tiki-taka" style of play, characterized by quick, short passing and maintaining possession. This style led to tremendous success for the club.

Atletico Madrid's Achievements: Atletico Madrid, traditionally considered the third major club in Spain, has won multiple La Liga titles and has been a strong contender in both domestic and European competitions.

Top Goal Scorer: Lionel Messi holds the record for the most goals in a single La Liga season. He scored 50 goals for Barcelona during the 2011-2012 season, surpassing Telmo Zarra's previous record.

Ligue 1

Inauguration: Ligue 1 was founded in 1932 under the name "National" and later changed to Ligue 1 in 2002.

Number of Teams: Ligue 1 typically consists of 20 teams competing for the league title each season.

Paris Saint-Germain Dominance: Paris Saint-Germain (PSG) is the most successful club in recent years, winning multiple Ligue 1 titles. They have also made a significant impact in European competitions.

AS Saint-Étienne's Historic Run: AS Saint-Étienne holds the record for the most consecutive Ligue 1 titles. They won the league title in an impressive run from 1967 to 1970.

Top Scorer: Delio Onnis holds the record for the most goals scored in Ligue 1. He scored 299 goals while playing for Stade de Reims and AS Monaco.

Highest Scoring Match: AS Monaco and FC Sochaux-Montbéliard played out the highest-scoring match in Ligue 1 history in 1935, with Monaco winning 8-6.

Ligue 1

French Derby Matches: Matches between PSG and Marseille, known as Le Classique, and matches involving AS Saint-Étienne, Lyon, and Lille are some of the most intense and historic rivalries in Ligue 1.

Monaco's Title-Winning Season: AS Monaco won Ligue 1 in the 2016-2017 season, ending PSG's streak of consecutive titles. Monaco scored a remarkable 107 goals that season.

Legendary Players: Ligue 1 has been home to legendary players like Zinedine Zidane, Thierry Henry, Michel Platini, George Weah, and many others who have left a significant mark on the league.

Famous Stadiums: Ligue 1 is played in iconic stadiums like Parc des Princes (PSG), Stade Vélodrome (Marseille), Groupama Stadium (Lyon), and Stade Louis II (AS Monaco).

Top Talent Development: Ligue 1 clubs are known for their youth academies, producing talents who often become stars not only in France but also in other top European leagues.

Bundesliga

Inauguration: The Bundesliga was founded in 1963, replacing the Oberliga as the top-tier football league in Germany.

Number of Teams: Bundesliga typically consists of 18 teams competing for the league title each season.

Borussia Dortmund and Bayern Munich Rivalry: Matches between Borussia Dortmund and Bayern Munich, known as Der Klassiker, are one of the most intense and watched football rivalries in the world.

Bayern Munich Dominance: Bayern Munich is the most successful club in Bundesliga history, having won multiple league titles. They have been particularly dominant in recent years, securing consecutive championships.

Top Scorer: Gerd Müller holds the record for the most goals scored in a single Bundesliga season. He scored 40 goals for Bayern Munich in the 1971-1972 season.

Borussia Mönchengladbach's Success: Borussia Mönchengladbach won five Bundesliga titles in the 1970s, making them one of the dominant clubs of that era.

National teams

World Cup

Brazil: Brazil has won the FIFA World Cup a record 5 times. The Brazilian national team is the only team to have appeared in every World Cup since the tournament's inception in 1930.

Germany: Germany has won the World Cup 4 times and has finished as runners-up 4 times as well. The German national team holds the record for the most goals scored in a World Cup match, beating Saudi Arabia 8-0 in 2002.

Argentina: Argentina has won the World Cup 2 times, with their most recent victory in 1986. Argentine legend Diego Maradona led his team to victory in the 1986 World Cup, a tournament in which he scored the famous "Hand of God" goal.

England: England won their only World Cup in 1966, when they hosted the tournament. The English Premier League is one of the most popular and competitive football leagues globally, featuring top clubs like Manchester United, Liverpool, and Chelsea.

National teams

World Cup

Spain: Spain won their first World Cup in 2010 in South Africa. Spain's national team is known for its "tiki-taka" style of play, emphasizing short passing and movement, which led to their success in international competitions.

France: France has won the World Cup 2 times, with their most recent victory in 2018 in Russia. The French national team is known for its multicultural composition, with many players having diverse backgrounds, reflecting the country's immigration history.

Portugal: Portugal won their first major international tournament, the UEFA European Championship, in 2016. Portugal is famous for having one of the greatest footballers of all time, Cristiano Ronaldo, who has set numerous records and won numerous individual awards.

El Salvador's Fastest Goal: El Salvador's Mágico González scored the fastest goal in World Cup history in 1982, finding the net just 49 seconds into a match against Hungary.

National teams

World Cup

Italy: Italy has won the World Cup 4 times, with their most recent victory in 2006. Italy is known for its strong defensive style of play, and their national league, Serie A, is considered one of the best football leagues in the world.

Cameroon's Memorable Debut: Cameroon became the first African team to reach the World Cup quarter-finals in 1990. Their attacking style and physical play left a lasting impression on fans worldwide.

Saudi Arabia's Quick Goals: Saudi Arabia holds the record for the fastest two goals scored in World Cup history. In the 2002 World Cup, they scored two goals in just 2 minutes and 14 seconds against Tunisia.

South Korea's Semi-Final Appearance: South Korea co-hosted the World Cup with Japan in 2002 and reached the semi-finals, becoming the first Asian team to achieve this feat. They finished in fourth place after losing to Turkey in the third-place playoff.

Players

Pele (Brazil): Pele is the only player to have won three FIFA World Cup titles: in 1958, 1962, and 1970. He scored over 1000 official career goals, a remarkable achievement.

Diego Maradona (Argentina): Maradona is famous for his "Hand of God" goal and the "Goal of the Century" in the 1986 World Cup quarter-final against England. He led Argentina to victory in the 1986 World Cup, securing their second title.

Johan Cruyff (Netherlands): Cruyff was a key player in popularizing the "Total Football" style of play. He won three Ballon d'Or awards and later became a successful manager, especially at FC Barcelona.

Franz Beckenbauer (Germany): Beckenbauer won the World Cup as both a player (1974) and a manager (1990), a unique achievement in football history. He was known for his defensive skills and ability to initiate attacks from the back, earning him the nickname "Der Kaiser."

Players

Cristiano Ronaldo (Portugal): Ronaldo has won multiple FIFA Ballon d'Or awards and is known for his goal-scoring prowess and athleticism. He has had successful stints with Manchester United, Real Madrid, and Juventus, among others.

Zinedine Zidane (France): Zidane scored twice in the 1998 World Cup final, helping France win their first World Cup title. He is known for his elegance on the ball and his playmaking abilities.

Johan Neeskens (Netherlands): Neeskens was a key player in the Dutch national team during the 1970s, known for his energy and versatility on the field. He played a significant role in the development of Total Football.

Lionel Messi (Argentina): Messi has won multiple FIFA Ballon d'Or awards, breaking the record for the most wins. He spent the majority of his club career at FC Barcelona, where he became the club's all-time leading scorer.

UK Players

Sir Bobby Charlton (England): Bobby Charlton was part of the England team that won the 1966 FIFA World Cup. He scored a record 49 goals for the English national team, a record that stood for almost half a century.

George Best (Northern Ireland): George Best was known for his incredible dribbling skills and was a crucial player for Manchester United during the 1960s and 1970s. Best won the Ballon d'Or in 1968, becoming the first Northern Irish player to achieve this honor.

Sir Stanley Matthews (England): Matthews played professional football until he was 50 years old, showing remarkable longevity in his career. He won the inaugural Ballon d'Or award in 1956 at the age of 41.

Ryan Giggs – Rugby Background: Before becoming a football star, Ryan Giggs, the legendary Welsh winger, was a talented rugby player. He played rugby league as a child before choosing football as his career.

Referees

Professional Training: Referees undergo extensive training to understand the rules of the game thoroughly. Many top-level referees are former players who transition to officiating after their playing careers.

Communication Skills: Referees must have excellent communication skills to interact with players, coaches, and officials effectively. They often need to diffuse tense situations on the field.

Vanishing Spray: Introduced in recent years, vanishing spray is used by referees to mark the spot for free-kicks and the defensive wall, ensuring players maintain the correct distance during set-pieces.

Goal-Line Technology: To determine if the ball has crossed the goal line, referees now use goal-line technology, which instantly informs them if a goal should be awarded.

Referee Signals: Referees have specific hand signals to indicate various decisions, such as fouls, advantages, and goal kicks. These signals help players and fans understand the referee's decisions.

Referees

Pierluigi Collina: Widely regarded as one of the greatest referees, Collina's piercing stare and bald head became iconic. He officiated the 2002 FIFA World Cup final between Brazil and Germany.

Howard Webb: Webb refereed the 2010 FIFA World Cup final between Spain and the Netherlands. He was also an English Premier League referee for many years, earning respect for his calm demeanor on the pitch.

Mark Clattenburg: Clattenburg officiated the finals of both the UEFA Champions League (2016) and the UEFA Euro 2016. He is known for his authoritative style and clear decision-making.

Nestor Pitana: Pitana, an Argentine referee, officiated the 2018 FIFA World Cup final between France and Croatia. He became the second referee in history to officiate both the opening match and the final of a World Cup in the same year.

BONUS Scandals

Calciopoli Scandal (2006): A match-fixing scandal in Italy involving top clubs like Juventus, Milan, and Lazio. Juventus was relegated, and several officials were banned.

FIFA Corruption Scandal (2015): High-ranking FIFA officials were arrested for corruption, leading to significant reforms within the organization.

Marseille Bribery Scandal (1993): French club Olympique de Marseille was involved in a match-fixing scandal leading to their Ligue 1 title being stripped.

The German Bundesliga Referee Scandal (2005): German referee Robert Hoyzer was found guilty of match-fixing and was banned for life. Several other referees and players were also implicated.

The Belgian Football Scandal (2018): Several Belgian clubs, including Anderlecht and Club Brugge, were investigated for match-fixing and fraud, leading to arrests and ongoing legal proceedings.

Printed in Great Britain
by Amazon

34196627R00046